RUSSELL DALGLEISH & WENDY SNEDDON

The Ask

How Smart Business Owners Get Support, Clients, and Opportunities

JFDI SECRETS
No excuses. Just action.

SCOTTISH BUSINESS NETWORK

First published by JFDI Secrets in conjunction with The Scottish Business Network 2025

First edition

ISBN: 978-1-0684945-0-5

This book was professionally typeset on Reedsy.
Find out more at reedsy.com

Contents

Acknowledgments

This book exists because of a community. **The ASK** is more than a concept, it's a practical tool shaped by the shared ambition, insight, and collaboration of people across the Scottish Business Network (SBN). Everyone who has been part of this global community has, in some way, contributed to the ideas captured here. I'm grateful to each of you.There are, however, a few people without whom this book would not have been possible.

First, my co-founder of SBN, Christine Esson. Your belief in me and in our mission has been a constant source of energy and purpose. Your partnership has fundamentally changed the direction of my life. This book is, in many ways, a result of what we've built together.

Second, Wendy Sneddon. You were the one who took the spark of "The ASK" and had the vision to codify it. This book exists because you made it happen. Your clarity, commitment, and talent have been vital from start to finish.

Finally, to our core team, Kendra, Scott, Ian, Steve, Jamie and Cath. You've been there from the beginning. Your commitment and drive are embedded in everything we've achieved.

Thank you all. My sincere hope is that this book will serve others as a guide, to help them learn from what we've done, and to go even further.

Thank you,
  Russell

Foreword

When Christine Esson and I first conceived SBN in 2016 our ambitions were simply to help connect Scottish based companies secure opportunities in London by gathering and mobilising the Scottish community in the UK's capital city.

Today we have over 100 Ambassadors across the world, 20,000 plus members of our community and representation in over 70.

This journey has been achieved through hard work, an incredible supportive community both at home and around the world and critically a coded methodology of how we deliver support.

We call it the "The ASK". We felt that by documenting how "The ASK" works we could help many more Scots and those with an affinity for Scotland based across our planet.

The ASK is our tried and trusted method for mobilising support for your business, to enhance your chance of success and to deliver to our global family members the opportunity to engage with you.

This is not a fancy sales technique or trick for making a quick buck. SBN is a non-profit, voluntary organisations built to help others. What we have developed with "The ASK" is a way to get you thinking that will allow you to mobilise the support we have created for you amongst our global supporters of Senior Execs, Policy Makers, Entrepreneurs and Investors.

This book is of course written with the Scottish business leader with international ambitions in mind but the techniques we describe will be of use to anyone with global ambitions.

Be sure to check us out at www.sbn.scot, follow us on LinkedIn and join of growing community. Membership is free and available to all.

Russell Dalgleish, Co Founder & Chair, SBN

Testimonial

At the heart of the Scottish Business Network is a belief that opportunity comes from connection.

'The ASK' empowers individuals to tap into the collective goodwill, experience and global reach of the Scottish diaspora — unlocking doors that might otherwise remain closed.

It's not just a method; it's a mindset that turns ambition into action."

— *Christine Esson, Co-Founder, Scottish Business Network*

I

Part One

1

The Global Growth Opportunity

Let's start with a question: Why not you?

Why shouldn't your business be the one making waves beyond borders? Why not have your product or service land in new markets, in front of new customers, with new streams of revenue coming in from cities you've only seen on a map? Because here's the reality: it's possible. More possible than you think. More importantly, it's happening right now for other small and medium-sized business owners just like you.

What stands between you and global growth usually isn't some massive obstacle. It's not a lack of talent or product quality. It's not even funding, in many cases. What's standing in the way is direction. Clarity. Connection. And that's exactly what this book, and this chapter, is here to kick-start.

The Myth of "Too Small to Go Global"

Too many business owners tell themselves they're not ready for international expansion. They think going global is for the big players. For the companies with legal departments, international offices, and ten-figure turnovers. But that myth is costing people opportunities. Today's world is hyper-connected. Supply chains are global. Customers are digital. People care more about authenticity, story, and value than whether your HQ is in a high-rise. The truth? If you've built something that solves a real problem or brings real value, someone out there is looking for it.

If you're Scottish, you've already got a competitive edge. Scottish business has a global reputation for trustworthiness, quality, and character. We're known for showing up, doing the job right, and adding a bit of charm along the way. That's currency in the global market.

So, What's the Holdup?

Here's what I've seen time and time again: business owners who *want* to grow but don't know how to take the leap. They're working long hours. They're spinning all the plates. They're wearing every hat in the company. The idea of tackling international growth, feels impossible when they're already stretched to the limit. Sound familiar? That's why this book exists. Because you don't need to go it alone. You don't have to have all the answers. You just need the right people in your corner, and it all starts with getting clear on what you need, **The ASK**.

The Global Opportunity Is Personal

This isn't about ticking boxes or hitting vanity metrics. This is about your life and your legacy.

Global growth means:

- Diversifying your revenue.
- Reducing dependence on one market.
- Creating jobs and opportunities for others.
- Getting recognised and respected outside your local scene.
- Building something you can pass down or exit from with pride.

Maybe you want to open a branch in Canada. Or find a distributor in Singapore. Maybe you're ready to partner with a like-minded company in Australia or bring your tech to Silicon Valley. No matter the shape of your dream, there's a path to get there. It begins with understanding that global isn't just for "them."

It's also for *you.*

The Importance of Community

No one succeeds globally in isolation. That's not how the world works. The most successful businesses out there are powered by networks. Behind every international breakthrough, there's a conversation, a connection, a relationship that opened a door. That's the role SBN plays. We don't just believe in Scottish businesses. We back them. We connect them to global Ambassadors, industry insiders, potential partners, mentors, and investors. We act as that missing link between ambition

5

and access.

But none of that can happen unless you step up and share your ambition. Unless you show up with a clear ASK.

Why This Book, and Why Now?

The timing has never been better. Technology has levelled the playing field. We can pitch investors over Zoom. Sign contracts with e-signatures. Ship goods across borders with precision and ease. And post-pandemic, there's a hunger for innovation, new partnerships, and resilience.

Scotland is already on the map for whisky; fintech; health tech; renewables; creative industries, you name it. If you're reading this, there's room for *you* on that list too.

This book will show you how to:

- Understand and define your ASK.
- Build relationships that matter.
- Tap into the SBN ecosystem.
- Connect with global Ambassadors.
- Create momentum in your international journey.

Every chapter is packed with real stories, practical tools, and simple but powerful strategies you can apply today. This isn't theory. This is a guide built from the lived experiences of business owners who were where you are and made the leap.

The Bottom Line

You're not too small. You're not too late. You're not under-qualified. You just need clarity, connection, and the courage to make an ASK.

So, ASK yourself:

- Where do I want my business to be 12 months from now?
- What does international success look like for me?
- Who do I need to talk to?
- What support do I need to make it happen?

That's the start of your global growth journey.

We're here to walk it with you. Let's get started.

2

Why "The ASK" Matters

Let me say it straight: if you don't know what to ASK for, no one can help you. You can walk into a room full of the most connected, generous, influential people in your sector, but if you just talk about your business without clearly saying what you need, nothing will happen. I've seen it. Again, and again.

You show up at a networking event or hop on a Zoom call. You do the usual intro: who you are, what you do, maybe even what makes you different. But when it comes to taking the conversation forward, when someone ASKs, *"How can I help?"* you freeze. Or worse, you say something vague like:

"I'm just looking to grow," or *"I'm open to opportunities."*

That's not an **ASK**. That's a conversation killer.

What Is "The ASK"?

The ASK is a specific, well-thought-out request that helps move your business forward. It could be:

- An introduction to someone in a particular market.
- A recommendation for a service provider in another country.
- A referral to a potential client or partner.
- Insights from someone who's already done what you're trying to do.
- Access to funding sources or advice on how to raise capital.

The ASK is what takes your story and uses this to power your business , to allow the universe to help you. When someone hears your ASK, they instantly know how they can help, and the clearer you are, the more likely they are to say, *"Yes, I know someone."*

The Cost of Not Asking

Let's flip it.
   What happens when you *don't* make an ASK?
   Nothing.

- Best-case scenario? You're remembered as a nice person with an interesting business.
- Worst-case? You're forgotten entirely.

Opportunities don't fall into your lap just because you show up. They come when you signal what you need. And let's be honest, people *want* to help, but they're busy. They need direction. Clarity cuts through the noise.

Why People Avoid The ASK

Here's what I've noticed: many business owners avoid Asking because they think it makes them look weak, needy, or pushy. But that's not how the real-world works. In fact, the opposite is true. People respect clarity. They respect vision. They respect a business owner, entrepreneur or founder who knows exactly what they need and isn't afraid to ASK.

The ASK shows ambition. It shows focus. It tells people, *"I'm not just here to mingle; I'm here to build."* Just to be absolutely clear: having an ASK doesn't mean you're *taking* from others. It means you're creating a space for others to contribute, to connect, to collaborate. It's a two-way street.

The SBN Experience

At SBN, we see this every day. The difference between a member who makes progress and one who doesn't? Nine times out of ten, it comes down to the ASK. I remember a member who spent weeks attending events, making connections, doing all the right things, except Asking for anything specific. The moment he started saying, "I'm looking for introductions to independent hotel chains in the Nordics," the response flipped. Emails came in. Calls were made. A month later, he had meetings booked. People didn't suddenly start liking him more. He just gave them a way to help.

Turning Talk Into Action

Here's what I want you to take from this book:

Every conversation is a chance to move forward, but only if you bring an ASK.

So, the next time you're at a networking event or having a coffee with a potential supporter, be ready. Don't just talk about what you do. Don't just talk about your vision. Talk about what you need. Be direct. Be specific. Be brave.

- *"I'm looking for a food distributor in Canada who works with independent retailers."*
- *"Do you know someone who's taken a health tech product into the US?"*
- *"I'm exploring Dubai as a market, can you connect me with someone who knows the retail space there?"*

When you show up with that kind of clarity, doors open.

Your Homework

Let's make this real. Here's what I want you to do right now:

1. Write down your top three business goals for the next 6-12 months.
2. For each goal, ASK yourself: What's stopping me from achieving this today?
3. Turn that barrier into a specific ASK using the **A S K** system.

A.S.K. System

Action – Stuck – Key

A – Action

- *Where are you trying to go? What are you trying to do?*
- What's your business goal right now? Be specific.
- Example: "Enter the German market."

S – Stuck

- *Where are you stuck? What's in your way?*
- What barrier is preventing progress? Be honest and clear.
- Example: "No local contacts or understanding of distribution channels."

K – Key

- *What is key to your success? What do you need to move forward?*
- Make the **ASK**. Say what you want, who you want it from, and why.
- Example: "I'm looking for introductions to food distributors in Germany who work with sustainable products."

Why It Works

- **A** gets you focused on the direction.
- **S** uncovers the real blocker (not just "growth," but *what's*

stopping it).
- **K** gives people a way to help, fast.

Now you've got something powerful. Something usable. Something memorable.

Final Thought

Having an **ASK** doesn't mean you're unprepared. It means you're serious. This chapter is short, but the impact is long-lasting. Because if you get this right, if you practice the habit of Asking clearly and confidently, you'll transform every networking opportunity, every conversation, and every relationship. You don't need to have it all figured out. But you do need to know what to ASK for next.

So, what's your **ASK**?

3

Meet Scottish Business Network (SBN)

If you're serious about growing your business beyond the local market, let me introduce you to one of the most powerful tools at your disposal: SBN. This isn't your average networking group. There's no awkward small talk. No plastic name tags and lukewarm coffee. What we've built is a dynamic, international network of Scots and friends of Scotland who are invested in helping businesses like yours go global.

Why SBN Exists

Let's be honest. Business can be lonely, especially when you've got global ambitions. You might be the only one in your circle thinking about exporting, setting up in a new country, or pitching to investors overseas. That isolation can stall your momentum. SBN was created to solve that. We exist to connect the dots for ambitious Scottish businesses. We connect people, ideas, and opportunities, and we do it across borders. Whether you're a solo founder or leading a growing team, if you've got a clear ASK, we've got someone who can help.

The People Behind the Network

At the heart of SBN is a core team who believe in the power of community-led growth. Together, we've helped hundreds of businesses gain traction globally, not with gimmicks or empty slogans, but by creating meaningful, practical connections.

The SBN Difference

So, what makes us different?

1. **Global Ambassadors:** We have a growing group of Ambassadors around the world. These are seasoned business leaders embedded in their local markets, from New York to Singapore, Dubai to Sydney. They're not figureheads. They're active, engaged, and looking to help.
2. **Strategic Introductions:** We don't just throw people into a directory and hope for the best. We take time to understand your business and your **ASK**, then make introductions that are targeted and useful.
3. **Collaboration Over Competition:** Our community doesn't operate on ego. It thrives on support. It's a place where people genuinely want to help each other succeed. That spirit is baked into everything we do.
4. **Events That Work:** Our online and in-person events are designed with one purpose: to help you connect in meaningful ways. Every event is a chance to sharpen your message, expand your network, and move one step closer to your goals.

How It Works for You

Here's how you can make the most of being part of SBN:

- **Join:** Start by becoming a member. It's simple, and it gets you into the ecosystem.
- **Show Up:** Attend events. Turn up with intention. Prepare your ASK.
- **Get Matched:** Talk to us about what you need. We'll introduce you to someone who can help.
- **Follow Up:** Build the relationship. Follow through. ASK again.

This is not a passive thing. You get out of it what you put in. But the support is there, and it's real.

Why We ASK About Your ASK

Everything we do revolves around one question: **What's your ASK?** Once we know what you're looking for, we can activate the network. We can connect you to people with market knowledge, sector expertise, or funding insights. We can pull resources together. We can get things moving. We can't do that if you're vague. But show up with a clear ASK? We're off to the races.

A Quick Success Snapshot

- A fintech company looking to understand U.S. regulatory hurdles was connected to a retired compliance officer in Boston, an SBN Ambassador. That single call saved them six months of research.
- A Scottish textile startup wanted to break into Japan. Through SBN, they connected with a fashion buyer in Tokyo. Within four months, they were fulfilling their first international order.
- A founder needed help preparing for an investment pitch. We connected her to another member who had just closed a round. Not only did she nail her pitch, but she also gained a mentor in the process.

Final Word

You don't have to do this alone. Global growth isn't about luck. It's about having the right people in your corner. SBN exists to make that possible. We've built the runway, now we need you to step up, be clear, and be ready to take off.

So again: What's your **ASK**?

4

The Power of Rapport

Let's make one thing clear: no one helps someone they don't trust. That's why before we even talk about your ASK, we've got to talk about rapport. In SBN, and in business in general, rapport is your golden ticket. It's the foundation of every meaningful connection. It's what turns polite conversations into real opportunities. It's what makes people remember you and want to help.

Why Rapport Matters

When someone trusts you, they stick their neck out for you. They forward your email. They make that intro. They invite you into rooms you didn't even know existed. But if there's no trust, there's no traction. That's just human nature. People do business with people they like. They support people who show up as real, honest, and engaged. That's why rapport isn't a "soft skill." It's a strategic asset.

Building Rapport: The Right Way

Let me be blunt: rapport isn't built by launching straight into your ASK. It's built by being human first. When you meet someone, whether at an SBN event, in a LinkedIn chat, or over coffee, lead with curiosity, not agenda. ASK questions. Listen. Share a bit of your story.

Start with:

- "Tell me how you got into this line of work."
- "What's keeping you busy right now?"
- "What's been your biggest win this year?"

These aren't filler questions. They're signals. They show you care that you're not just there to take. When people feel heard, they open up. That's the moment real conversation starts, and real trust begins to form.

What Rapport Isn't

It's not fake flattery. It's not nodding your head while thinking about your own talking points. It's not schmoozing or saying yes to everything.

Rapport is genuine interest. It's connection rooted in shared values or goals. It's about building a relationship, not just making a transaction.

SBN in Action: The Rapport Effect

Let me give you an example. One of our members, a tech founder, joined an SBN call and didn't say a word about his business in the first ten minutes. He just listened, Tasked others about their work, and offered feedback where he could. By the end of the call, three people wanted to introduce him to potential partners, without him even Asking. Why? Because he came across as someone worth helping. That's the power of rapport. It makes people want to help before you even make an **ASK**.

Rapport First, ASK Second

This is the order that works:

1. Build rapport.
2. Understand the other person.
3. Share your story.
4. Make your **ASK.**

When you skip the first three steps, your **ASK** often lands flat. But when you build trust first, your **ASK** has context. It feels earned.

Practical Rapport Tips

Here are a few things that work:

- **Be present:** Put your phone down. Make eye contact (even over Zoom).
- **Follow up:** Send a thank-you message or a note about something they mentioned.
- **Be helpful:** If you can connect someone or share a resource, do it, even if there's nothing in it for you.
- **Stay consistent:** Show up to events regularly. Familiarity breeds trust.

What Happens Next

Once you've built rapport, everything changes. People remember you. They reply to your messages. They invite you into opportunities. Most importantly? They listen when you share your **ASK**. By then, you're not just another name, they know you, they trust you, and they want to see you succeed. So, the next time you meet someone through SBN or in any business setting, don't rush the pitch.

Start with rapport. It's not just polite. It's powerful.

5

Stories from the SBN Network

Real Business. Real People. Real Results.

You've heard me talk about the power of having a clear ASK. You've heard me say that connections can open doors, *if* you know how to knock. But don't just take my word for it. Let's look at what actually happens when business owners like you get specific, step up, and use SBN for what it was built for: connection, collaboration, and global growth. These stories aren't fairy tales. They're real. And they all started with someone deciding to speak up, to ASK, and to trust the process.

Whisky Meets Hamburg

From Local Pride to International Shelf Space: Let's talk whisky. Beautiful product. Strong story. World-class quality. But all that means nothing if it's sitting in a warehouse waiting for buyers to magically appear. One of our members, a small, independent whisky producer, had that problem. Passionate founder, great branding, solid domestic sales. But they wanted to break into

Germany and had zero contacts. At one of our events, they shared a simple, powerful ASK:

"I'm looking for introductions to distributors in Germany who understand premium spirits and work with independent brands."

That was it. That clarity made it easy for us to help. We connected them with our Ambassador in Hamburg, who knew the spirits space well. Within weeks, a conversation started with a boutique distributor. Fast-forward three months: shelf space secured, first shipment delivered, and early signs of traction. They didn't need a miracle. They needed the right intro, and they got it because they Tasked.

Tech Meets U.S. Capital

From Ambition to Funding: A young tech founder came to us with a powerful idea: a SaaS platform that improved on boarding for remote teams. They had early traction in the UK but needed capital to scale. Their ASK?

"I'm looking for investor introductions, ideally people in the U.S. who understand B2B SaaS."

Our team immediately identified three warm contacts in New York through our network of Ambassadors. One of those intros led to a meeting, which led to a an interest in investment. This founder didn't waste anyone's time. They didn't show up saying, "We need money." They came with data, a pitch, and a clear ASK. That's why they got results.

23

Health Meets Mentorship

Confidence is Contagious: A female entrepreneur building a health-focused product had hit a wall. She wasn't looking for funding (yet). What she really needed was mentorship, someone who'd walked her path and could help her navigate the mental blocks and business decisions ahead. Her **ASK**?

"I'm looking for a mentor who's scaled and exited a health business. Ideally someone who gets the challenges of being a woman founder in this space."

She connected with me directly. I knew exactly who to reach out to, one of our Ambassadors who had founded, grown, and sold two health businesses. Within one conversation, the match was made. What changed? Everything. Her confidence grew. She started pitching differently. She landed two new contracts in the months following. And yes, she's now preparing for investment. Sometimes, the right **ASK** isn't about money. It's about mindset.

Clean Tech Meets Middle East

Playing the Long Game: Let's not pretend this always happens overnight. One clean tech business came to us with a big goal: expansion into the Middle East. They had a proven product, a sustainability mission, and scalable infrastructure. What they didn't have was insight into the region. Their **ASK**?

"We're looking for someone in the UAE who understands public-sector procurement and sustainability goals."

We introduced them to our Dubai-based Ambassador, an ex-corporate strategist with deep government contacts. This wasn't a quick win. But over the following year, through multiple conversations, the business got a clearer roadmap and three opportunities to pilot their solution in local projects. This is what real global expansion looks like: patience, persistence, and partnership.

Bringing Scottish Fitness to the United States

When brothers Joe and Tony Burns founded Burns Gym, their mission was simple: improve the quality of life for elderly residents in care homes through fun, engaging fitness programmes — proudly delivered wearing traditional Scottish kilts. By 2025, they had grown their virtual fitness model to reach over 300,000 homes across the UK. But they weren't finished. They had a bigger ambition: international expansion, starting with the United States.

Knowing they couldn't break into the US market alone, they leveraged SBN to sharpen their focus and make critical connections. Their ASK was clear:

"We are seeking introductions to healthcare organisations and senior living facilities across the East Coast who could benefit from our live virtual fitness sessions."

With SBN's support, the Burns brothers participated in a trade mission to Florida and joined Tartan Week in New York. Through introductions facilitated by SBN Ambassadors, they secured meetings with key stakeholders in the care sector and delivered their first US-based session at Carnegie East House, an assisted living facility in New York.

The response was overwhelmingly positive, validating their model for the American market. Burns Gym is now actively securing its first US clients, a major milestone in their global expansion journey.

Their success shows the power of having a focused ASK, and trusting the network to help open the right doors.

What These Stories Have in Common

Let's break it down:

1. **Clarity:** Every single one of these businesses came with a clear, specific ASK. Not "I want to grow," but "I need *this person* in *this place*."
2. **Courage:** Asking takes guts. You have to be honest about what you don't have and ASK someone for help. That's vulnerable, and it's also powerful.
3. **Follow-through:** After the ASK comes the work. These founders showed up, followed up, and did the hard yards after the introduction was made.

And because of that? They got results.

This Could Be You

You're reading this for a reason. Maybe you've got an idea. Maybe you've hit a ceiling. Maybe you're sick of going it alone. Whatever your situation is, here's what I want you to hear:

You don't need to do it all yourself. But you do need to ASK.

SBN is here. We have the relationships. We have the knowledge. We've built this ecosystem for people exactly like you, entrepreneurs with global ambition and local roots. So, when you're ready to move forward, don't hold back. **ASK like it**

matters. Because it does. Your story could be the next one we tell.

6

Understanding Your ASK

Clarity is your superpower

By now, you've heard the word "**ASK**" enough times to know it's important. But let's get practical, because knowing you need an **ASK** and knowing how to craft one are two very different things. Too many business owners stall right here. They believe in the idea, but when it comes time to say it out loud, clearly, confidently, they hesitate. Maybe they don't want to come across as too direct. Maybe they're not sure what's realistic. Maybe they're just overwhelmed. So, this chapter is your how-to. Your blueprint. Let's break it down and get you to a place where you're not only *ready* to make your **ASK** but you're excited to.

Why You Need to Understand Your ASK

Imagine you walk into a room full of people who genuinely want to help you grow your business. But when someone says, "So, what are you looking for right now?" you freeze. You mumble something about growth or collaboration and leave the conversation with a polite nod and nothing else. That moment right there? That's your opportunity vanishing. Understanding your **ASK** means you can take full advantage of moments like that, whether it's a networking event, a one-to-one meeting, or even a casual LinkedIn comment thread. Your **ASK** is the bridge between your ambition and the people who can help you get there.

Keep it simple, here are a few ways to pull together what you need for your **ASK.**

The A.S.K. System
Action – Stuck – Key

A – Action

- *Where are you trying to go? What are you trying to do?*
- What's your business goal right now? Be specific.
- Example: "Sell my products in Dubai."

S – Stuck

- *Where are you Stuck? What's in your way?*
- What barrier is preventing progress? Be honest and clear.
- Example: "No local contacts or understanding of distribution channels."

K – Key

- *What is the key to your success? What do you need to move forward?*

- Make the **ASK**. Say what you want, who you want it from, and why.
- Example: "I'm looking for introductions to business owners in Dubai who work with sustainable products."

Why It Works

- **A** gets you focused on the direction.
- **S** uncovers the real blocker (not just "growth," but *what's stopping it*).
- **K** gives people a way to help, fast.

The Four-Part Framework

Let's build your **ASK** with this simple framework:

Where are you now? Get real. No fluff. No inflated numbers. Just a clear, honest snapshot of your business.

- What's your current revenue?
- How big is your team?
- What markets are you in?
- What traction do you have (sales, clients, partnerships)?

Knowing where you stand is the first step to understanding what you actually need next. Example: *"We're a Dundee-based tech startup with £300K in revenue, serving clients in the UK education sector."*

Where do you want to go? This is your vision, but short-term, not some five-year pipe dream.

- Are you trying to enter a new market?
- Are you raising investment?
- Are you launching a new product line?

Focus on what's right in front of you over the next 6–12 months. Example: *"We want to expand into the Irish market and onboard our first five clients there this year."*

What's stopping you? Here's where you identify the blocker. This isn't about blaming the economy or competitors. This is about identifying the specific gap that's holding you back.

- Is it a lack of local contacts?
- Is it a lack of experience in that market?
- Are you unsure of regulations, pricing, partnerships?

Get focused on the *actual* challenge. Example: *"We don't have any connections in the Irish education sector and don't understand the procurement process."*

What do you need? This is your **ASK**. This is what you say out loud in the meeting, in the email, or at the end of your pitch.
It should be:

- Specific
- Actionable
- Easy to understand

Example: *"I'm looking for an introduction to someone in the Irish education space who can advise on procurement or help us access our first pilot schools."*

Now that's something people can respond to.

Let's Do It Together

Let's take another example and build it in real time.

Scenario: You run a Scottish eco-packaging company.

Where are you now?

"We're based in Edinburgh, with £500K in annual sales and two distribution partners in the UK."

Where do you want to go?

"We want to start exporting to the Nordic region in the next 12 months."

What's stopping you?

"We don't know who the key buyers or distributors are, and we don't have market insight into what sustainability standards are expected there."

What do you need?

"I'm looking for introductions to packaging distributors or sustainability consultants based in Sweden or Norway who understand retail supply chains."

That **ASK** is specific. It's realistic. And it opens doors.

Avoid These Common Mistakes

Let's clean up a few messy habits that weaken your **ASK**:

1. Being too vague

✕ "I'm looking to connect with people abroad."

✓ "I'm looking to meet HR Directors from companies who specialise in the food and drink Industry in London."

2. Making it too broad

✕ "We're open to anything."

✓ "Right now, we're focused on finding a mentor with experience in scaling digital services into Asia."

3. Asking for too much

✕ "I want someone to fund, mentor, and help me launch internationally."

✓ "I'm looking for someone who's done this before and can review our market entry plan."

You can always make more than one **ASK** over time. Don't cram everything into one breath.

When Your ASK Evolves

Here's the thing: your **ASK** will change, and that's a good sign. It means you're growing. You might start by needing local contacts, then later need funding, and after that, help with scaling operations or leadership coaching. Keep refining as your business matures. A good rule of thumb: every quarter, revisit your ASK. ASK yourself:

- Has anything changed?
- Is my ASK still aligned with my current focus?
- Do I need to update people in my network?

Your Turn

Let's put it into action. Take a few minutes to write these out:

1. Where are you now?
2. Where do you want to go in the next 6–12 months?
3. What's standing in your way?
4. What's your **ASK**?

Write it. Practice saying it. Try it in conversations. Post it on LinkedIn. Use it in meetings. This is your tool, and it works when you use it.

Final Thought

Understanding your **ASK** isn't about having all the answers. It's about knowing your next step and giving others a chance to help you take it. People can't support a business they don't understand. And they can't act on an **ASK** they can't hear clearly. So do yourself a favour: take the time to get this right.

Be clear. Be specific. Be brave.

Your next opportunity might just be waiting on the other side of that **ASK**.

7

Building Your Pitch

Crafting an introduction that connects, converts, and gets you the help you need.

By now, you know the importance of your ASK, but here's the missing piece most people overlook: the way you introduce yourself makes or breaks your ASK. You're not just Asking for help. You're Asking for attention, action, and trust. That starts with how you show up. We're not talking about a stiff elevator pitch. You need a **pitch:** a short, powerful introduction that sets the tone, communicates your value, and lands your ASK clearly.

The 5-Part Formula for a Memorable Pitch

You'll use this structure every time you network, present, or even post online.

1. Who do you serve?

This sets the context. Tell people who your product or service is for. Be specific.

"I work with independent food producers across Scotland."

Not: *"We serve everyone."* No, you don't. Get laser-focused.

2. What do they want or need?

This shows you understand your market. What problem are you solving?

"They want to grow into international markets but struggle with logistics and market insight."

Now you've got attention, because this is relatable.

3. What results do they get?

What's the outcome of working with you?

"Our clients typically secure export partnerships within six months and double their overseas revenue within a year."

If you don't tell people what your work *achieves*, you're just another business.

4. Where will you find them?

This helps others help you. It's subtle positioning. You're signalling who you're trying to meet.

"We're focused on connecting with buyers and distributors in the Nordic region."

This primes your audience to start scanning their network for relevant contacts.

5. Who are you? What's your ASK?

This is your close. Keep it sharp. Say who you are and what support you need *right now.*

"I'm Jamie, founder of Nordic Naturals. I'm looking for introductions to sustainable product distributors in Sweden or Norway."

Boom. That's your full pitch.

Pulling It All Together

Here's how the full pitch sounds when it flows:

"I work with independent food producers across Scotland. They want to grow into international markets but struggle with logistics and market insight. Our clients typically secure export partnerships within six months and double their overseas revenue within a year. Right now, we're focused on buyers and distributors in the Nordic region. I'm Jamie, founder of Nordic Naturals, and I'm looking for introductions to sustainable product distributors in Sweden or Norway."

See what we did there?

- Built rapport by showing who we help and how.
- Created credibility with results.
- Ended with a focused, direct **ASK**.

You could sharpen up further starting with a hook:

"If you're an independent food brand looking to break into international markets but don't know where to start, I get it. That's exactly who we help. I'm Jamie, founder of Nordic Naturals. We help Scottish producers expand globally, fast. Most of our clients land export partnerships in under six months and double overseas revenue within a year. Right now, we're focused on the Nordics and looking for intros to sustainable product distributors in Sweden or Norway. Know anyone I should speak to?"

Why This Works

This 5-part system isn't just simple, it's **effective**. Why?

- It gets to the point.
- It shows you know your business and market.
- It makes it easy for someone to say, "I know someone you should speak to."

And best of all? It's conversational. It doesn't feel like a pitch, it feels like purpose.

Common Mistakes to Avoid
"We work with anyone."
You lose people when you're vague. Specificity sells.
"We offer lots of things."
Great. But right now, what's the *one thing* you're Asking for?
"We're just hoping to grow."
Hope isn't a strategy. Be clear about what kind of growth, where, and with whom.

Practice Makes Powerful

Write your 5-part pitch. Then practice it until it feels natural. Say it out loud. Use it on LinkedIn. Drop it in meetings. Lead with it when someone ASKs, *"So what do you do?"* This isn't just about networking. This is about showing up as someone who knows what they're doing, who they're doing it for, and what they need next.

Final Thought

If you take nothing else from this chapter, remember this:

"Be memorable. Be clear. Be bold with your **ASK**."

The people who get the most from their network are not the most experienced, they're the ones who show up ready to ASK for something real.

Now, take the 5-part pitch framework and make it yours.

8

Using the SBN Ecosystem

This is your global launchpad, use it.

You've defined your ASK. You've built your pitch using the 5-part formula. Now it's time to plug in, to use SBN like the powerful resource it is. SBN isn't a magic button. It's a high-trust, high-impact network of people who want to help, but they can only help if you show up and use the ecosystem with purpose. Let's walk through exactly how to do that.

What Is the SBN Ecosystem?

Think of SBN as a well-connected global community with one goal: **Helping Scottish businesses grow internationally.**
  It's made up of:

- **Events (online and in-person):** Where connections start.
- **Partners:** Selected business partners with VIP status
- **Global Ambassadors:** People on the ground in key markets who open doors.

- **One-to-One Intros:** Facilitated by the core team to get you in front of the right people.
- **LinkedIn Power:** A high-trust digital community that actually pays attention.
- **Supportive Members:** Founders, investors, and professionals who know what it's like to need help, and want to give it.

But here's the catch: you need to engage. This isn't *"sign up and wait."* This is *"show up, speak up, and follow up."*

How to Actually Use the Ecosystem

1. Start with Events. But Go in Prepared

When you attend an SBN event, online or in person, don't go in blind. Know your **ASK**. Have your pitch ready. Be prepared to say it in 30 seconds or less. When someone says, *"Tell me about your business,"* don't waffle. Lead with purpose. Be just as curious about *them*. Great networkers give first, ASK second.

2. Get Yourself on the Radar

This means being visible: Create a profile on the SBN platform or website. Follow and engage with SBN and its leaders on LinkedIn. Comment thoughtfully. Share useful posts. Re-share events or opportunities. People help people they recognise. Stay visible and valuable.

3. Book One-to-Ones Intentionally

Don't wait for introductions to fall in your lap. Be proactive. Reach out to the SBN team and say: *"Here's my ASK. Who should I be speaking to in the network?"* Even better: suggest a target.

"I'd love to speak to someone who's scaled into Australia or who understands SaaS investment in the U.S." These won't be cold intros, they're warm, curated, and made with intention. Use them.

4. Tap into the Global Ambassadors

This is one of the most powerful assets of the SBN ecosystem. These are people embedded in local markets: New York; Singapore; Dubai; Toronto; etc; who understand the business landscape in their respective countries. They can introduce you to distributors, investors, or partners. They will translate market expectations and save you months of wasted time and effort. But they're not mind readers. You need to show up with a clear **ASK** and a clear value proposition. Respect their time. Deliver your pitch. Be specific. Then follow through.

5. Use LinkedIn Like a Pro

This is where most of the magic happens between events. Post your pitch. Share your **ASK** publicly. Tag people (respectfully). Comment on others' posts with generosity. Here's an example:

"We're looking to connect with clean-tech buyers in Scandinavia. Do you know someone in your network who works in sustainable energy procurement? Our results show cost savings of 40% within the first year, happy to share a case study."

Keep it short. Clear. And give people a reason to say "yes."

Be the Person People Want to Help

Let's be blunt. If you show up once, ASK big, then disappear, you'll be ignored next time. But if you show up consistently, contribute, and help others first, people will remember you.

- Want intros? Make some.
- Want support? Offer yours.
- Want engagement? Give it first.

That's how networks work.

Common Mistakes in the Ecosystem

Here's what not to do:

- **Being passive:** This isn't a membership site. It's a living, breathing community.
- **Spamming people with generic pitches**: Always personalise. Always be human.
- **Not following up:** If someone makes an intro, reply. Show gratitude. Keep them in the loop.
- **Failing to refine your ASK:** What worked last month may not be your focus now. Keep updating your pitch.

Your Ecosystem Action Plan

Let's simplify this. Here's your checklist:

1. Join the SBN network (online or locally).
2. Write your pitch using the 5-part method.
3. Attend the next event and *use* your pitch.
4. Reach out to an Ambassador or team member with a clear **ASK**.
5. Post your ASK on LinkedIn once a week.
6. Make three helpful introductions for others in the network.
7. Follow up with anyone who helps you. Every time.

43

Final Thought

SBN is a community, not a directory. It only works when you do. You've got the tools now. You've got the language. You've got the network. Now use it. Show up. ASK clearly. Follow up consistently. Help others first. That's how you turn one connection into a global opportunity.

9

Connecting with Global Ambassadors

You bring the ASK. They bring the access.

Here's the part too many people miss: you don't need to go global alone. SBN is full of people who've already been where you want to go. We call them Global Ambassadors. They're not just figureheads or advisors. They're real business leaders, on the ground, plugged into their local ecosystems, and they're here to help you. But they can't help if you don't reach out. And they won't help if you're vague. This chapter is all about how to connect with them the right way: with respect, purpose, and a crystal-clear ASK.

Who Are the Global Ambassadors?

SBN's Global Ambassadors are senior-level professionals, business owners, and experienced entrepreneurs based in major cities and regions around the world. They've built companies, sat in boardrooms, led expansions, and navigated markets you're only just eyeing. They're based in places like:

- New York
- Singapore
- Dubai
- Toronto
- Sydney
- Hong Kong
- Amsterdam
- San Francisco

These aren't just locations they're doorways into new business landscapes. The people behind them are here for one reason: to help Scottish businesses grow internationally. But here's the golden rule:

You bring the ASK. They bring the access.

What a Good Connection Looks Like

A successful conversation with a Global Ambassador isn't a monologue or a sales pitch. It's a two-way conversation. You're not just there to talk about yourself, you're there to *ASK smart questions*, share your specific challenge, and be open to learning.

Here's what a strong approach looks like:

"Hi, I'm Anna, founder of Eco Wraps. We produce biodegradable packaging and are ready to expand into the UAE. I'm looking for guidance on how local procurement works and whether there's appetite for sustainable products in food retail. Would you be open to a 20-minute chat to share your insight?"

See what she did?

- She introduced herself quickly.

- Named the business and product clearly.
- Gave a specific region and goal.
- Named her **ASK**: insight and feedback.

You don't need to impress. You need to be honest and direct. That's what gets traction.

What They Can Help With

Every Ambassador is different, but here's the kind of support they can typically offer:

- **Market intel:** Cultural nuances, sector insights, business etiquette.
- **Warm introductions:** To buyers, investors, mentors, legal advisors, or agencies.
- **Reality checks:** Telling you what *won't* work as much as what will.
- **Referrals:** To people in their network who've done what you're trying to do.

They won't write your strategy or sell your product. But they'll help you avoid mistakes, move faster, and connect smarter.

How to Approach an Ambassador

Let's keep this simple. Here's a checklist for your outreach:

1. **Be respectful:** They're busy. Don't ASK for an hour of their time. ASK for 15–20 minutes.
2. **Be prepared:** Know your **ASK**. Know your pitch. Don't show up rambling.
3. **Be curious:** ASK them about the market. What works? What doesn't?
4. **Be specific:** *"I want to grow in Asia"* is vague. *"I'm targeting Singapore's retail sector"* is actionable.
5. **Be generous:** If you see a way to support *them,* do it. Share their content. Connect them with someone. Collaboration goes both ways.

Don't Make These Mistakes

- Asking for vague help like *"I'm just hoping to connect."* That tells them nothing.
- Pitching your full business deck before they ASK. Start a conversation, not a pitch.
- Ignoring their advice. If they challenge your assumptions, listen.
- Not following up after. If someone helps you, keep them updated. It shows respect and builds trust.

Examples of How It's Done

Example 1: Fintech in NYC

A fintech founder wanted access to angel investors in the U.S. She connected with an SBN Ambassador in New York with experience in early-stage finance. After a brief intro call, she was invited to pitch at a virtual investor showcase and landed a key meeting the next week.

Example 2: Food Brand in Singapore

A premium snack brand founder reached out to an Ambassador in Singapore Asking for guidance on shelf placement and buyer relationships. They were introduced to a retail consultant, and within six months had their first test order.

Example 3: SaaS Expansion into Canada

One founder thought he needed investment, but the Canadian Ambassador helped him see he first needed a local reseller partnership. That redirection saved him six months of chasing funding he didn't need yet.

Your Turn

If you haven't already, visit www.sbn.scot and complete our online form. Draft your **ASK**. Write a short, respectful message introducing yourself. Send it. We will respond to you within 48 hours. Prepare your 5-part pitch. Don't overthink. Don't wait for perfection. We are here because we *want* to help you.

Final Thought

You don't grow globally by accident. You grow when you connect, when you ASK, and when you follow through. So, reach out. The world is waiting. One conversation with the right person in the right market could change everything. Let's bring it all together and map your next move.

10

Next Steps: Your Growth Map

You've got the tools. Now build the plan.

You've done the thinking. You've got the **ASK**. You know how to show up, pitch for support, and tap into SBN. But let's be honest, none of that matters if you don't take action. This chapter is your Growth Map. Not a theory. Not a daydream. A real, practical, step-by-step plan to help you move forward with purpose. Whether you're just getting started or you're ready to scale into your second or third international market, this is your moment to commit.

Step 1: Connect with the Network
Start here: **Have you already joined the SBN community?**

- If yes, great. Introduce yourself with your refined pitch.
- If not, go to www.sbn.scot and register.

Then attend the next event, virtual or in-person. Get visible.

Be present. And don't lurk, show up with your **ASK** ready to go. This isn't about collecting business cards. It's about starting meaningful conversations that lead to action.

Step 2: Finalise Your pitch
You've seen the 5-part structure:

1. Who do you serve?
2. What do they want or need?
3. What results do they get?
4. Where will you find them?
5. Who are you, and what are you Asking for?

Write it down. Practice it. Say it in front of a mirror. Record yourself. Get feedback. Post it on LinkedIn and see what responses you get. It should roll off your tongue when someone says, *"So, what do you do?"*

Step 3: Reach Out With Intention
Start with these three actions:

1. **Send a message to one Global Ambassador.**Introduce yourself. Share your pitch. ASK for a short call.
2. **Email an SBN team member.**Say what you're trying to do and ASK for a relevant intro or event suggestion.
3. **Post your ASK publicly.**Use LinkedIn or another platform where your audience is active. Include your **ASK** clearly. Tag SBN if relevant.

This is the "**ASK**" part in action. If you stay quiet, you'll stay stuck.

Step 4: Build Relationships, Not Just Leads

This isn't spray-and-pray marketing. This is personal connection, focus on quality, one solid relationship can unlock a market. Be curious, ASK about others. Help when you can, share useful content. Connect people who should meet, this builds trust, and trust builds opportunity. Remember: your next investor, partner, or mentor is one introduction away. Be the kind of person people want to introduce.

Step 5: Refine and Repeat

Your ASK isn't static. It evolves as your business grows. So, keep refining it.

Set a monthly review:

- What's changed in your business?
- Is your ASK still the same, or has your next barrier shifted?
- Who in your network can help now?

Make this a habit. Review, adjust, re-ASK. You're not being repetitive. You're being strategic.

Your 30-Day Growth Challenge

Here's a checklist to guide your next month:

WEEK 1

- Finalise your 5-part pitch
- Post your **ASK** on LinkedIn
- Attend one SBN event
- Contact 5 people in your network every day and start building rapport.
- Arrange a 1-1 every day

WEEK 2

- Reach out to at least one Global Ambassador
- Schedule a one-to-one with someone in your industry
- Share someone else's **ASK** publicly
- 5 A Day & 1-1 A Day

WEEK 3

- Follow up with anyone who offered support
- Share a small win or update publicly
- Offer to help another SBN member
- 5 A Day & 1-1 A Day

WEEK 4

- Review your **ASK**: has anything changed?
- Make a list of 5 new people to arrange 1-1s with for next

month
- Thank everyone who supported you this month
- 5 A Day & 1-1 A Day

Follow this roadmap, and you'll do more than just grow.
You'll build a reputation. A rhythm. A pipeline of opportunity.

Final Note

Here's the truth: global growth isn't reserved for big brands or flashy startups. It's for you, if you're willing to **ASK**, to act, and to keep showing up. The SBN ecosystem is here. The Ambassadors are ready. The support is available. But the next step? That's yours to take.

II

ASKs

This section shows a selection of real-world examples of clear, powerful Asks in action, from entrepreneurs seeking investor introductions, to non-profits securing sponsors, to business owners unlocking partnerships. Each story illustrates how defining exactly what you need, to get what you want.

11

Nexus.scot

Combating Age Bias: Connecting Experience with Opportunity

ACTION

What are we doing — where are we trying to go?

Nexus.scot is a national organisation tackling the persistent age bias that sidelines talented senior professionals once they reach their 60s, despite having decades of invaluable leadership, industry knowledge, and networks. Our mission is to position Nexus.scot as **the leading connector for senior executives seeking fractional, interim, advisory, and portfolio roles**, while simultaneously helping businesses plug critical strategic gaps with proven experience, fast.

Right now, our goals are to:

- Grow and diversify our **network of client businesses**, from ambitious scale-ups to established firms managing growth, succession, or transformation.

- Expand our **pool of highly accomplished senior executives** ready to step in as interim leaders, advisors, or board contributors.
- Raise awareness of the powerful value senior expertise brings to organisations needing to steady the ship, accelerate growth, or navigate complex change.

STUCK

How are we stuck? What's in our way?

We have a strong foundation: an impressive pool of seasoned leaders, a clear proposition, and a growing reputation. But our biggest barrier is **direct access to the right decision-makers,** CEOs, board members, and HR leaders, especially those who may not yet realise the competitive advantage that flexible senior talent can deliver. Without stronger direct connections and trusted partnerships with businesses and industry bodies:

- We risk missing the chance to showcase how an interim or fractional executive can transform a business's growth trajectory.
- We lose time and momentum in building the national recognition needed to challenge outdated biases about age and leadership.
- We limit the number of high-impact matches we can make between exceptional people and businesses that need them.

KEY — Our ASK

Our ASK is simple but powerful: **Introductions to CEOs,**

board members, senior HR decision-makers, and industry association leaders who:

- Understand that experienced fractional interim or advisory leadership can solve pressing business challenges cost-effectively.
- Want to future-proof their organisations with diverse, battle-tested strategic thinking.
- Are open to exploring flexible engagement models, whether it's filling an urgent C-suite gap, adding niche expertise, or strengthening governance through a portfolio NED role.

Who we need it from:

- **Connectors** across executive search, professional networks, board communities, chambers of commerce, and industry associations.
- **Mentors, advisors, and business leaders** who know which organisations are ready for this conversation, and can open the door.

Why now?

The market for experienced, flexible leadership is growing fast. Economic uncertainty, rapid digital transformation, and succession planning pressures all mean businesses need **trusted, agile senior talent** more than ever, but they don't always know where to look.

Nexus.scot is poised to become the **go-to solution** for this challenge, but only if we can scale our connections and amplify our reach in the next 12 months.

Outcome so far:

Where we have made warm introductions, we've seen rapid wins, securing interim placements, advisory roles, and valuable board contributions that have delivered immediate impact for clients *and* proven the case for tackling age bias head-on. Each introduction compounds our reputation and demonstrates the powerful economic and social benefit of putting experience back at the heart of business strategy.

A S K at a glance

A — "Scale Nexus.scot to become the UK's trusted hub for interim, advisory, and portfolio placements that unlock the overlooked value of senior executive experience."

S — "We lack warm connections into mid-market and larger businesses that would benefit most from flexible senior support but haven't yet tapped into this resource."

K — "We're asking for introductions to CEOs, board chairs, HR directors, or industry bodies that champion innovative leadership models and want to work with proven, credible experts."

Who from: Trusted connectors within professional networks, boardrooms, industry groups, or those with direct access to decision-makers.

Why now: We're ready to scale, and every door opened helps us combat age bias while delivering immediate value to UK businesses.

Outcome: Early introductions have already resulted in multiple successful placements, repeat client engagements, and a growing network of advocates committed to reshaping how businesses think about experience, value, and flexible senior leadership.

If you can open a door, you can change the conversation. Let's unlock the potential of experienced leaders **together**. Connect with us at www.nexus.scot

12

Harry Lauder: The Musical — Celebrating Legacy, Raising Impact

ACTION

"Lauder: The Musical" was a one-night-only theatrical celebration of Sir Harry Lauder's extraordinary legacy, the Scottish music hall superstar who rose from humble beginnings to become the world's highest-paid entertainer of his day, and who dedicated his fame to supporting British troops during WWI and beyond. Our goal was to position this show as a **premier cultural and philanthropic event in London**, honoring Lauder's story of resilience, laughter, and service, while raising crucial funds for **Erskine Veterans Charity**, Scotland's foremost veterans' care organisation. This special event:

- Shone a spotlight on a legendary Scottish entertainer whose story still resonates today.
- Brought together Scottish diaspora, London's theatre lovers, veterans' supporters, and new audiences under one roof.
- Directly benefited veterans through all proceeds and part-

nerships with Erskine.

STUCK
What's blocking our progress?

While we have an incredible story, a talented creative team, and the partnership with Erskine in place, our biggest challenge is **limited reach beyond niche theatre-goers and existing Scottish heritage circles**. Without broader promotion and corporate/philanthropic backing:

- Ticket sales may not reach capacity, limiting funds raised for Erskine.
- We risk missing corporate sponsorship opportunities that could amplify the event's profile and impact.
- We lose the chance to engage influential cultural and veterans' communities who would naturally champion this cause.

KEY (ASK)

Following the London launch, we plan to expand "Lauder: The Musical" as a touring production, taking this inspiring story and its charitable mission to audiences across the UK. Our **ASK** is clear: **Introductions, connections, and support from individuals and organisations** who care about any of the following:

- Scottish heritage and cultural storytelling
- Supporting veterans and military families
- Philanthropic community and corporate social responsibility (CSR)
- The London theatre scene and unique cultural events

Specifically, we're seeking:

- **Corporate sponsors** with CSR interests in heritage, the arts, or veterans' welfare.
- **Cultural ambassadors** and Scottish diaspora leaders in London who can champion the event.
- **Media partners** to tell the story behind the show and its impact.
- **Community influencers and networks** to help spread the word and reach new audiences.

This event is not just a show, it's the start of something bigger: a touring celebration that keeps Sir Harry Lauder's legacy alive *while directly supporting veterans for years to come.*

Outcome so far:

Where warm introductions have already been made, senior executives with Scottish connections, particularly ex-military, have proven to be passionate champions. They've offered promotional support, opened sponsorship conversations, and committed to bringing their networks to the performance. This is exactly the multiplier effect we need.

A S K — at a glance

A - *Launch "Lauder: The Musical" as a flagship cultural event in London celebrating Sir Harry Lauder's legacy while raising significant funds for Erskine Veterans Charity.*

S - *Our current audience is mostly theatre-goers and Scottish heritage supporters — we need wider reach and stronger sponsor engagement to scale ticket sales and impact.*

K - *We're asking for introductions to corporate sponsors, cultural/-media partners, Scottish diaspora influencers, and veterans' sector supporters who can amplify our reach and impact.*

Join Us — Champion Legacy, Support Veterans

If you can help open a door, share an introduction, or sponsor this unique evening, please get in touch with www.sbn.scot

Together, we can ensure Sir Harry Lauder's legacy inspires, and makes a difference, for generations to come.

13

QA Solutions — Your Trusted Remote Outsourcing Partner

ACTION

What are we doing? Where are we trying to go?

QA Solutions is a remote outsourcing organisation based in Lahore, Pakistan. Since 2018, we've specialised in helping small- and mid-sized enterprises (SMEs) unlock scale and efficiency through reliable, cost-effective outsourcing solutions.

Our mission is to position QA Solutions as a **preferred, value-driven outsourcing partner** for SMEs worldwide — particularly in the UK, US, and other English-speaking markets — who need trusted, high-quality virtual support to free up their core teams and accelerate growth.

We offer a **broad, flexible service portfolio**, including:

- Executive virtual assistance
- LinkedIn lead generation and outreach
- Content creation & social media management
- Graphic design & web development
- Appointment setting and back-office support

With an experienced team, competitive pricing, and a culture of integrity and accountability, QA Solutions is designed to act as an **extension of our clients' teams**, so they can focus on what they do best.

STUCK
How are we stuck? What's in our way?

We have the capacity, the systems, and the proof of concept, but our biggest challenge is **low brand visibility and limited direct access to decision-makers in target markets**.

SMEs that need virtual talent often struggle to find trusted off-shore partners, but they're unlikely to discover us without warm referrals, credible endorsements, or trusted intermediaries who can bridge the trust gap.

- We compete in an overcrowded BPO marketplace with limited marketing spend.
- We can't demonstrate our proven value to enough founders and business owners who would benefit from our services.
- We lose opportunities to grow sustainably through word-of-mouth, the most powerful channel for high-trust outsourcing relationships.

KEY — Our ASK
What do we need to unlock progress?

Our **ASK** is for introductions with trusted intermediaries who already serve growth-focused SMEs, such as:

- Business mentors and startup coaches
- Marketing consultants and agency networks
- Startup incubators and accelerator programmes

- Professional services firms or VCs with portfolio companies in need of scalable remote talent
- Online business communities with SME founders

Why now?

We have:

✔ Five years of proven delivery across multiple sectors

✔ Strong client references and adaptable service packages

✔ A skilled, growing team ready to take on more complex and larger-scale assignments

Now is the right time to **scale through trusted partnerships**, ensuring we grow sustainably while delivering exceptional value to clients and referrers alike.

Outcome so far:

Early pilots with local and international clients have validated our service quality and built a strong operations base. Initial champions and introducers helped us open key doors, from there, we rapidly built a sales pipeline with high conversion rates. This demonstrates that **referral-led growth is our best-fit model for scale**.

A S K — at a glance

A — "Grow QA Solutions into a trusted multi-service remote outsourcing partner for SMEs in the UK, US, and beyond, giving business owners back their time and focus."

S — "We lack direct brand visibility and warm referral pathways into international SME networks, making client acquisition slower and more resource-heavy than it needs to be."

K — "We're asking for introductions to potential partners, referrers, or trusted co-marketing channels, business mentors, incubators, agency networks, or startup accelerators, who can connect us with founders ready to scale through reliable outsourcing."

Let's help more SMEs grow, together, visit www.qasolutionsbpo.com

14

Engineer a Career — Inspiring the Next Generation of Engineers

ACTION

Engineer a Career is a Glasgow-based non-profit dedicated to inspiring, informing, and guiding the next generation of engineers from diverse backgrounds. We connect students, graduates, and career changers with real stories and practical advice through our fast-growing podcast series, live events, and partnerships with local educators and industry role models. Our goal is to expand our reach across Scotland and the UK, building on the success we've achieved locally to engage engineering communities nationwide. We want to partner with universities, colleges, professional institutions, and employers to open up more pathways and opportunities for young people who might not see themselves as future engineers — yet!

In the next 12 months, we aim to:

- **Double our podcast audience** and launch themed series with leading employers.
- **Host regional live events** in at least 5 major UK cities.
- Develop **mentorship and volunteering opportunities** connecting students with practicing engineers.
- Build a national network of supporters who champion engineering careers for all.

STUCK

While our local engagement has been strong, with packed live events, positive press coverage, and word-of-mouth support, we currently face a major barrier: limited national visibility and lack of formal partnerships with large employers and institutions. Without these national connections:

- It's harder to secure funding and sponsorship for bigger events.
- We can't reach new student audiences outside our local area.
- We miss out on the chance to spotlight diverse engineering employers who want to stand out as places where new talent belongs.

KEY

What do we need to unlock progress?

To accelerate our national growth, our **ASK** is for **warm introductions to engineering companies and industry bodies** who want to build their future workforce and raise their profile among ambitious young people.

Specifically, we're looking for:

Contacts inside **large engineering companies** — talent leads, CSR teams, early careers managers — who want to:

- Co-host podcasts or branded live events.
- Get involved in mentorship opportunities.
- Sponsor outreach that positions them as an employer of choice.

Connections to **industry bodies or professional institutions** that could support us in taking our events and podcast to a national stage.

Why now?

Our podcast downloads and event waiting lists show the appetite is there. We have a proven, scalable model — but we need the right partners to amplify our impact and build momentum.

Outcome so far:

Already, early introductions have resulted in volunteers stepping forward to share their stories and networks, creating a powerful ripple effect. With your help, we can multiply this impact and ensure young people everywhere see engineering as an exciting, achievable path.

A S K — at a glance

- **A** — *"We're scaling Engineer a Career UK-wide — inspiring the next generation of engineers through podcasts, live events, and partnerships."*
- **S** — *"We lack national-level awareness and partnerships with big employers to make this happen at scale."*
- **K** — *"Could you introduce us to decision-makers in engineering*

companies or industry bodies who want to stand out as top employers for emerging talent?"

If you can help us make connections, **get in touch** at www.engin eeracareer.co.uk or drop us a message. Together, let's build a brighter future for UK engineering.

15

The Ultimate Ask: Russell Dalgleish

For many of us the most important "Ask" we will make in our lifetime is the moment when, on one knee, we ask our partner to become our wife.

Action: To ask the women I love to commit the rest of her life as part of an exclusive partnership with me.

Stuck: While I know what I want to say and the emotion I'm feeling, I'm unsure how to phrase everything in a simple yet deeply personal way, and how to plan the setting so it feels authentic, not pressured or overdone.

Key:
My ASK is:

- Help crafting a personal, meaningful proposal script that captures our story, the qualities I love in her, our future vision, and ends with the question, "Will you marry me?"
- Guidance on choosing the right setting that has emotional

resonance, aligns with her comfort level (intimate vs. public), and matches her personality.
- Advice on logistics, such as discreet ring presentation, considering and minimising stress.

Who I need it from:

- Trusted friends or family who know her well.

Why now:

I feel ready to take the next step in our relationship. This proposal marks a pivotal moment, and I want it to be memorable in an authentic, loving way, one we'll cherish forever.

Example in A.S.K. Format:

- A — "Formalise my life commitment by proposing marriage in a moment that's heartfelt and meaningful."
- S — "I'm uncertain how to structure my words and orchestrate the moment so it feels genuine and intimate, rather than overthought or scripted."
- K — "I'd like help writing my proposal speech based on our shared experiences, guidance on selecting a setting she'll feel comfortable with, and logistical advice (ring handling, capturing the moment, timing)."

OutCome: After taking on board as much advice as I could I chose Paris as the location and the Eiffel tower as the perfect spot. She said "yes" and we have now been married for 36 years so I can safely say the approach worked

III

Summary

16

Final Thoughts

One ASK away. That's all it takes.

Let's cut through the noise: you're not stuck because your business isn't good enough. You're not stuck because you lack talent, ambition, or a big enough dream. You're stuck because you haven't Tasked for what you really need. It's that simple, and that hard. We live in a world where help is everywhere, but it doesn't find you. You have to go get it. And that starts with knowing what to ASK for and having the courage to say it out loud. This book has given you the framework. The mindset. The tools. But none of it means a thing if it stays on these pages. This Isn't About Confidence, it's About Clarity. You don't need to be the most confident person in the room. You just need to be the clearest. Clarity makes people lean in. It makes introductions easy. It makes help automatic.

So when someone ASKs, *"How can I help you?"* Be ready.

- Don't say, *"I'm just looking to grow."*
- Say, *"I'm looking for a distribution partner in Canada who works with boutique wellness brands."*
- Don't say, "I'm open to opportunities."
- Say, "I'm looking for a mentor who's scaled a B2B service business into Europe."

Clarity is what turns a friendly chat into a business-changing connection.

Courage Is the Differentiator

You might worry about sounding needy, or pushy, or "not ready." Let that go. Every person who's grown a global business has asked for help. They've Asked for intros, for advice, for second chances, and warm leads. The only difference is, they Asked. If you want to grow, if you want to expand into new markets, if you want to be part of the global business conversation, you must be willing to speak up. Don't wait until you're 100% ready. The truth? No one is.

Connection Is the Strategy

Forget cold calling. Forget doing it all alone. The shortcut is already built, and it's called SBN. Use it. Lean into it. Be part of it. This isn't just about finding clients. It's about finding partners, champions, mentors, and collaborators. People who genuinely want to help you, if you let them. You don't need a huge team. You don't need millions in funding. You need the right few people who believe in what you're doing. You'll find them. But you have to speak.

What Happens Next?

Here's your final checklist:

- Know your ASK.
- Build your pitch.
- Join the SBN network.
- Show up to events.
- Reach out to Ambassadors.
- Share your ASK online.
- Help others.
- Keep As King.
- Keep growing.

This isn't a one-off campaign. It's a way of operating. A habit. A mindset. When you show up with clarity and courage, the right people notice. They respond. They help. If this sounds daunting, or maybe you want help to develop and refine your **ASK** – maybe that's your **ASK**, you can join our mastermind and get coaching and support from our team.

A Final Word from Me

I've worked with thousands of business owners, from those just starting out to those breaking into international markets. Every success story I've seen has one thing in common: They Asked. They Asked for help. For guidance. For support. For introductions. For truth. For feedback. For belief. So let this be your turning point. No more silence. No more playing small. ASK clearly, ASK often. Your next investor, distributor, mentor, or partner? They're already out there. They're just one **ASK** away.

To find out more about SBN and craft your ASK please visit:
www.TheASK.scot or **www.SBN.scot**

17

WORKSHEET — THE A.S.K. SYSTEM

A — ACTION *What are you doing - where are you trying to go?*

· My clear business goal right now is:

S — STUCK *How are you stuck? What's in your way?*

· The specific barrier that's stopping me is:

K — KEY *What do you need to unlock progress?*

· My ASK is:

Example:
A — "Enter the German market."
S — "No local contacts or distribution knowledge."
K — "I'm looking for introductions to food distributors in Germany who work with sustainable products."

18

WORKSHEET — THE 5-PART PITCH

What results do your clients get when they work with you?
The outcome for my clients is:

Who do you serve?
My customers are:

What do they want or need?
The big challenge I solve is:

Where will you find them?
I'm focused on this market/location:

Who are you + what's your ASK?

I am: _____

My ASK is: _____

_____

_____

_____

_____

_____

_____

Example:

"We help our clients secure export partners in 6 months. I work with Scottish eco-packaging firms who want to expand into the Nordics but lack distribution contacts. I'm Jamie from Nordic Naturals — I'm looking for introductions to sustainable product distributors in Scandinavia."

☑ Write it out.

☑ Practice it aloud.

☑ Use it in meetings, networking, or online.

☑ Get what you want.

Russell Dalgleish, Co-Author of The ASK

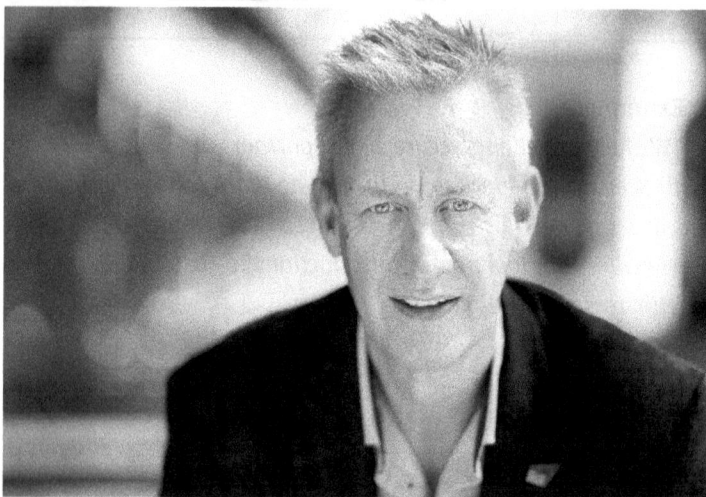

Russell Dalgleish

Russell Dalgleish is a globally respected business leader, se-
rial entrepreneur, and passionate advocate for Scottish entrepreneurship. As the co-author of *The ASK*, Russell brings
decades of real-world insight into how business owners can
unlock growth and opportunity, by learning to ASK the right
question, at the right time, to the right people.

With a career that spans executive roles in international business, angel investing, and innovation advisory, Russell is best known as the founding chair of the Scottish Business Network (SBN), a global community of Scottish entrepreneurs, investors, and leaders committed to helping Scottish companies expand into international markets. Under his leadership, the SBN has grown into a powerful platform for connection, collaboration, and global opportunity, with a strong emphasis on practical support, introductions, and real-world results.

Russell's journey started in the tech industry, where he held senior executive positions in international companies, including technology integrators and software firms. From there, he transitioned into entrepreneurship and investment, co-founding multiple businesses and advising countless startups and SMEs on how to scale successfully. His hands-on experience, combined with his vast global network, has positioned him as one of the most connected and influential figures in the Scottish business ecosystem. A government and policy makers advisor, and a leading voice on LinkedIn.

A sought-after speaker, mentor, and strategist, Russell is regularly invited to share his expertise on leadership, growth strategy, and international expansion. He has delivered keynote speeches on stages from New York to Dubai, championing the potential of Scottish businesses on the global stage. His core belief—that the world is full of people willing to help, but we must first learn to make a clear and confident *ASK* is the foundation of this book.

The ASK is not just a book; it's a movement. And Russell's role in it is crucial. He has spent years helping entrepreneurs articulate what they really need, be it funding, partners, advice, or visibility and then guiding them to the people and platforms that can help them achieve it. His ability to open doors, broker meaningful connections, and challenge business owners to think bigger has made him a transformational figure in countless success stories.

Russell's contributions to business have not gone unnoticed. He has been named one of the UK's Top 100 Entrepreneurs, serves as a non-executive director for several high-growth companies, and continues to mentor early-stage founders through accelerators and innovation hubs.

Through *The ASK*, Russell shares what he has learned at every level of business: that opportunity often lies just one question away. His voice throughout the book is one of optimism, practicality, and empowerment — encouraging business owners not just to dream, but to act.

Whether you're looking to expand overseas, attract investment, or simply get better at building your network, Russell's insights will inspire you to step forward and *ASK*. http://russell dalgleish.com

Wendy Sneddon, Co-Author of The ASK

Wendy Sneddon is an accomplished business strategist, author, and champion for small business owners who want to grow with confidence, clarity, and purpose. As co-author of The ASK, Wendy brings a fresh, practical perspective shaped by years of experience supporting entrepreneurs to unlock their voice, own their value, and take bold steps toward their goals.

Wendy is an ambassador for the SBN and the founder of JFDI

Secrets Ltd, a business dedicated to helping entrepreneurs, especially those in service-based industries, write and publish books that position them as credible experts in their field. She believes passionately that every business owner has a powerful story to tell, and that sharing that story can be the key to attracting the right clients, building trust, and growing a thriving business.

Her career began in HR and learning & development, where she supported leaders to build stronger teams, develop communication skills, and implement people strategies that drive results. This background gave her a deep understanding of the internal barriers that hold business owners back — like imposter syndrome, lack of focus, or the inability to articulate their value and inspired her mission to change that.

Wendy's signature approach is simple but powerful: stop hiding, get clear on your message, and just ASK. This philosophy runs through every aspect of The ASK, which she co-authored to demystify the process of reaching out for help, building partnerships, and stepping into the spotlight.

In The ASK, Wendy shares tools, stories, and frameworks designed to help small business owners ASK for what they need, whether it's support, investment, introductions, or visibility. She knows from experience that most entrepreneurs are brilliant at what they do, but struggle to communicate their worth or ASK for help without feeling like they're failing. Her mission is to flip that script and empower people to see Asking not as a weakness, but as a strength.

Wendy is also the editor of www.sentinel.scot, a Scottish business publication that celebrates innovation, entrepreneurship, and community. She uses the platform to spotlight the people and organisations driving change across Scotland and beyond, while giving others the tools and encouragement to share their own stories.

As a business coach, author and speaker, Wendy has helped business owners move from self-doubt to self-published.

With The ASK, Wendy has brought together her expertise in business growth, personal development, and storytelling to create a practical guide that anyone can use. Her voice throughout the book is supportive, straight-talking, and up-lifting, reminding readers that their next opportunity could be just one ASK away.

Whether you're starting out, scaling up, or looking to make a bigger impact, Wendy Sneddon will inspire you to step up, speak out, and ASK for what you truly want. https://www.linkedin.co m/in/wsneddon